This edition was produced by the Publishing Division of Campbell Soup Company, Campbell Place, Camden, NJ 08103-1799.

Corporate Editor:	Pat Teberg
Assistant Editors:	Alice Joy Carter,
	Gloria J. Pinchac,
	Margaret Romano
Senior Marketing Manager:	Brent Walker
Public Relations Manager:	Donnalyn Pompper
Campbell Kitchens:	Nancy DeBenedetta
Photography:	Peter Walters Photography,
	Chicago, IL
Photographers:	Peter Walters, Peter Ross
Photo Stylist/Production:	Betty Karslake
Food Stylists:	Lois Hlavac,
	Moisette McNerney,
	Gail O'Donnell,
	Carol Parik

Designed and published by Meredith Custom Publishing Services, Locust at 17th Street, Des Moines, IA 50336. Printed in Hong Kong.
First Trade Paperback Edition 1996.

Pictured on the front cover, clockwise from top right: Savory Chicken and Mushrooms (page 36), Broccoli-Cheese Potato Topper (page 38) and Classic Green Bean Bake (page 12).

Preparation and Cooking Times: Each of these recipes was developed and tested in the Campbell Kitchens by professional home economists. Use "Prep Time" and "Cook Time" given with each recipe as guides. The preparation times are based on the approximate amount of time required to assemble the recipe *before* baking or cooking. These times include preparation steps, such as chopping; mixing; cooking rice, pasta, vegetables; etc. The fact that some preparation steps can be done simultaneously or during cooking is taken into account. The cook times are based on the minimum amount of time required to cook, bake or broil the food in the recipes.

Campbell's BEST-EVER RECIPES

125th Anniversary Edition

THE COMFORT OF CAMPBELL'S SOUP FOR 125 YEARS

Never underestimate the power of soup! Through good times, fun times and especially mealtimes, Campbell's has been bridging the taste of time for 125 years.

The famous red and white Campbell's soup can was a symbol of goodness to generations of Americans long before Andy Warhol turned it into a pop art icon.

In the comfort of Campbell's, the world has taken part in an exciting, eventful journey that began in 1869 when Joseph Campbell and Abram Anderson formed a partnership to can fruits, vegetables, jellies and condiments. In 1897, a young chemist named Dr. John T. Dorrance joined the company and made a mark on world history with the invention of condensed soup. By reducing the water in canned soup, costs for packaging, shipping and storage were lowered. This made it possible to offer a 10½-ounce can of *Campbell's* Soup for a dime, versus about 30 cents for a typical 32-ounce can of soup. As a result, prepared soups once found mainly on upper-class tables became available to almost everyone and could also be used as a practical and delicious cooking ingredient. This one simple invention literally changed the way America eats.

Other creations under the Campbell banner have also become historic. In 1904, artist Grace Gebbie Drayton created the rosy-cheek *Campbell Kids*. Their appeal to both children and adults was enormous. The cherubic *Kids* are still among America's most recognized characters.

Campbell's: the taste of time... the taste of home. It is this kind of contemporary and "heartfelt marketing" that has kept the savory wholesomeness and relevance of *Campbell's* Soup on America's mind, on America's tables and even in the mess kits of America's servicemen and women around the world.

Campbell's Soup has cheered us through the Great Depression, warmed us through the Cold War and calmed us through the cultural and social currents that ultimately deliver us to a milestone anniversary where we are proclaiming the many benefits of soup. Campbell's is a quintessential American tradition 125 years in the making—and still being made.

Today, *Campbell's* Soups, and Campbell brands such as *Franco-American, V8, Campbell's* Tomato Juice, *Prego, Marie's* and *Pepperidge Farm,* are important ingredients in the lifestyles of every kind of family whose typical Sunday through Saturday now amounts to "life in the fast lane."

The recipes in this 125th anniversary cookbook are both new recipe ideas for the hectic 1990s and time-tested favorites updated and streamlined for quick and easy preparation. Enjoy these savory "greatest hits" and celebrate with us 125 years of *M'm! M'm! Good!* cooking.

*N*ow You're Cooking

What's in a name? If it's Campbell Soup Company, then "soup" really is our middle name! While Campbell's Soups include almost any type and variety imaginable—be it in our *Chunky, Home Cookin', Healthy Request,* or microwave soup lines—an estimated 440 million cans of condensed Campbell's Soup alone are used in recipes each year. The first Campbell cookbook, "Helps For The Hostess," was published in 1916 and showed homemakers how cooking with condensed soup eliminated the need for extra recipe ingredients to create appetizing and easy meals for entertaining.

During World War II, shortages and food rationing sharply reduced promotions for cooking with soup. But in 1948, Campbell opened new test kitchens and home economists began creating now-classic recipes such as Green Bean Bake, Glorified Chicken Bake, Souper Meat Loaf, Savory Pot Roast and Tomato Soup-Spice Cake.

THE CAMPBELL KIDS FIRST APPEARED ON A SERIES OF STREETCAR ADVERTISING CARDS IN 1905 AND WERE AN IMMEDIATE SENSATION WITH CHILDREN AND ADULTS ALIKE. GRACE GEBBIE DRAYTON, THE ORIGINATOR OF THE ROSY-CHEEK CHILDREN, REPORTEDLY MODELED THEIR FEATURES AFTER HER OWN.

AN EARLY LABEL FROM THE JOSEPH CAMPBELL PRESERVE COMPANY.

The convenience, ease and consistent good taste of these popular recipes using condensed soup remain as important to cooks today as ever.

1935 ADVERTISEMENT

1945 *The Saturday Evening Post* ADVERTISEMENT

1895   1897   1898   1993

SOUPER FACTS

In a recent national survey, 81 percent of all men and 79 percent of all women selected soup as the most comforting of all foods.

Frank Sinatra's contracts often specify that cans of Campbell's Chicken with Rice soup and a hot plate be in his dressing room prior to performances.

1913 ADVERTISEMENT

Campbell Soup Company sells more than 700,000 tons of soup each year...enough to fill the ocean liner, the Queen Elizabeth II, more than 10 times.

1992 Campbell's
soup poster

Advertisement, circa 1950

Campbell's First magazine
advertisement, *Good
Housekeeping*, 1905

1943 Advertisement

1924 Advertisement

❧

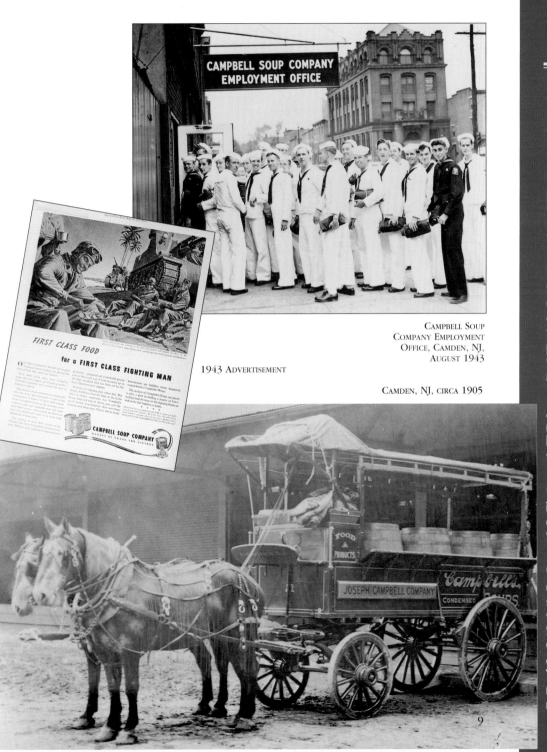

CAMPBELL SOUP COMPANY EMPLOYMENT OFFICE, CAMDEN, NJ, AUGUST 1943

1943 ADVERTISEMENT

FIRST CLASS FOOD

for a FIRST CLASS FIGHTING MAN

CAMDEN, NJ, CIRCA 1905

CAMPBELL SOUP COMPANY

9

What main course holds the distinction of being a convenience food, a comfort food, a tradition and a gourmet food all at the same time? It's meat loaf, a tasty time-honored classic whose evolution never stops. Why? Because people keep rediscovering it and reinventing it! In homes and eateries in every part of the country, meat loaf made with soup is a singular sensation that has earned a permanent place at America's table.

1935
ADVERTISEMENT

BEST-EVER MEAT LOAF

1 can (10¾ ounces) CAMPBELL'S condensed Tomato *or* Cream of Mushroom Soup
2 pounds ground beef
1 pouch CAMPBELL'S Dry Onion Soup and Recipe Mix
½ cup dry bread crumbs
1 egg, beaten
¼ cup water

- In large bowl, mix thoroughly *½ cup* tomato soup, beef, onion soup mix, bread crumbs and egg. In 2-quart oblong baking dish, *firmly* shape meat mixture into 8- by 4-inch loaf.
- Bake at 350°F. for 1¼ hours or until meat loaf is no longer pink (160°F. internal temperature). Spoon off fat, reserving *1 to 2 tablespoons* drippings.
- In 1-quart saucepan over medium heat, combine remaining tomato soup, water and reserved drippings. Heat through, stirring occasionally. Serve with meat loaf. If desired, serve with *green beans, roasted onions* and *cherry tomatoes.*

MAKES 8 MAIN-DISH SERVINGS	PREP TIME: 10 MINUTES COOK TIME: 1 HOUR 20 MINUTES

CLASSIC GREEN BEAN BAKE

1 **can (10¾ ounces) CAMPBELL'S condensed Cream of Mushroom Soup**
½ **cup milk**
1 **teaspoon soy sauce**
   Dash pepper
2 **packages (9 ounces *each*) frozen green beans, cooked and drained *or* 2 cans (about 16 ounces *each*) green beans, drained (4 cups)**
1 **can (2.8 ounces) French fried onions**

- In 1½-quart casserole, combine soup, milk, soy sauce and pepper. Stir in beans and ½ *can* onions.
- Bake at 350°F. for 25 minutes or until hot and bubbling; stir.
- Top with remaining onions. Bake 5 minutes more.

CORN AND BEAN AMANDINE

Prepare Classic Green Bean Bake as directed above, *except* substitute 1 can (10¾ ounces) CAMPBELL'S condensed *Golden Corn Soup* for the Cream of Mushroom Soup. Stir in ¼ cup toasted *slivered or sliced almonds* after baking 25 minutes. Top with remaining onions. Continue baking as directed. If desired, garnish with *fresh oregano* and *plum tomato*. *(Pictured opposite.)*

BROCCOLI BAKE

Prepare Classic Green Bean Bake as directed above, *except* substitute 1 can (10¾ ounces) CAMPBELL'S condensed *Cream of Broccoli Soup* for the Cream of Mushroom Soup and 1 package (20 ounces) *frozen broccoli cuts or 4 cups fresh broccoli flowerets* (about 1 bunch), cooked and drained, for the green beans.

MAKES ABOUT 4½ CUPS OR 6 SIDE-DISH SERVINGS	PREP TIME: 10 MINUTES COOK TIME: 30 MINUTES

MACARONI AND CHEESE

**2 cans (10¾ ounces *each*) CAMPBELL'S condensed
 Cheddar Cheese Soup**
1 soup can milk
2 teaspoons prepared mustard
¼ teaspoon pepper
4 cups hot cooked corkscrew macaroni (about 3 cups dry)
2 tablespoons dry bread crumbs
1 tablespoon margarine *or* butter, melted

- In 2-quart casserole, combine soup, milk, mustard and pepper; stir in macaroni.
- In cup, combine bread crumbs and margarine. Sprinkle over macaroni mixture.
- Bake at 400°F. for 25 minutes or until hot and bubbling. If desired, garnish with *carrot flowers* and *fresh germander mint.*

MAKES ABOUT 6 CUPS OR 8 SIDE-DISH SERVINGS	PREP TIME: 20 MINUTES COOK TIME: 25 MINUTES

CHEDDAR CHEESE SAUCE

**1 can (10¾ ounces) CAMPBELL'S condensed
 Cheddar Cheese Soup**
⅓ cup milk

- In 1-quart saucepan, combine soup and milk. Over low heat, heat through, stirring often. Serve over hot cooked vegetables, French fries or omelets.

MAKES ABOUT 1½ CUPS SAUCE	PREP TIME: 5 MINUTES COOK TIME: 5 MINUTES

CAMPBELLED EGGS

1 **can (10¾ ounces) CAMPBELL'S condensed Cheddar Cheese**
   or **Cream of Chicken Soup**
8 **eggs**
   Dash pepper
2 **tablespoons margarine *or* butter**

- In medium bowl, stir soup until smooth; gradually beat in eggs and pepper.
- In 10-inch skillet over low heat, melt margarine. Pour in egg mixture. As eggs begin to set, stir lightly so uncooked egg mixture flows to bottom. Cook until set but still very moist. If desired, garnish with *parsley.* Serve immediately.

Makes 4 Main-Dish Servings	Prep Time: 10 Minutes
	Cook Time: 15 Minutes

CLASSIC TUNA NOODLE CASSEROLE

1 **can (10¾ ounces) CAMPBELL'S condensed Cream of Celery**
   or **Cream of Mushroom Soup**
½ **cup milk**
2 **cups hot cooked medium egg noodles (about 2 cups dry)**
1 **cup cooked peas**
2 **tablespoons chopped pimento, optional**
2 **cans (about 6 ounces *each*) tuna, drained and flaked**
¼ **cup shredded Cheddar cheese (1 ounce), optional**
2 **tablespoons dry bread crumbs**
1 **tablespoon margarine *or* butter, melted**

- In 1½-quart casserole, combine soup and milk. Stir in noodles, peas, pimento and tuna.
- Bake at 400°F. for 20 minutes or until hot; stir.
- In small bowl, combine cheese, bread crumbs and margarine. Top tuna mixture with bread crumb mixture. Bake 5 minutes more.

Makes About 5½ Cups or 4 Main-Dish Servings	Prep Time: 15 Minutes
	Cook Time: 25 Minutes

SOUPERBURGER SANDWICHES

1 **pound ground beef**
1 **medium onion, chopped (about ½ cup)**
1 **can (10¾ ounces) CAMPBELL'S condensed Cheddar Cheese**
     or **Cream of Celery Soup**
1 **tablespoon prepared mustard** *or* **2 tablespoons ketchup**
⅛ **teaspoon pepper**
6 **hamburger buns, split and toasted**

- In 10-inch skillet over medium-high heat, cook beef and onion until beef is browned and onion is tender, stirring to separate meat. Spoon off fat.
- Stir in soup, mustard and pepper. Reduce heat to low. Heat through, stirring occasionally. Serve on buns.

Makes About 3 Cups or 6 Main-Dish Servings	Prep Time: 5 Minutes Cook Time: 15 Minutes

SHORTCUT SLOPPY JOES

1 **pound ground beef**
1 **can (11⅛ ounces) CAMPBELL'S condensed Italian Tomato Soup**
¼ **cup water**
2 **teaspoons Worcestershire sauce**
⅛ **teaspoon pepper**
6 **hamburger buns** *or* **Kaiser rolls, split and toasted**

- In 10-inch skillet over medium-high heat, cook beef until browned, stirring to separate meat. Spoon off fat.
- Stir in soup, water, Worcestershire sauce and pepper. Reduce heat to low. Heat through, stirring occasionally. Serve on buns.

Makes About 3 Cups or 6 Main-Dish Servings	Prep Time: 5 Minutes Cook Time: 15 Minutes

A popular variation of the hamburger is a cooked mixture of all the traditional ingredients, spooned onto a sandwich bun. Such seasoned ground beef mixtures became popular in the 1950s and 1960s, and are still called Souperburgers, Skillet Burgers, Coney Burgers or Sloppy Joes.

ONION-GLORIFIED CHOPS

1 **tablespoon vegetable oil**
1 **medium onion, sliced and separated into rings**
   (about ½ cup), optional
6 **pork chops, each ¾ inch thick (about 2 pounds)**
1 **can (10¾ ounces) CAMPBELL'S condensed Cream of Celery**
   or **Cream of Mushroom Soup**
¼ **cup water**

- In 10-inch skillet over medium-high heat, in hot oil, cook onion and *half* of chops 10 minutes or until browned on both sides. Remove onion and chops; set aside. Repeat with remaining chops. Pour off fat.
- In same skillet, combine soup and water. Heat to boiling. Return onion and chops to skillet. Reduce heat to low. Cover; cook 10 minutes or until chops are no longer pink, stirring occasionally. If desired, serve with *salad* and *grapes*.

MAKES 6 MAIN-DISH SERVINGS	PREP TIME: 5 MINUTES COOK TIME: 35 MINUTES

GLORIFIED CHICKEN BAKE

2 **pounds chicken parts**
1 **tablespoon margarine *or* butter, melted**
1 **can (10¾ ounces) CAMPBELL'S condensed**
   Cream of Chicken & Broccoli *or* Cream of Chicken Soup

- In 2-quart oblong baking dish, arrange chicken. Drizzle with margarine. Bake at 375°F. for 30 minutes.
- Spoon soup over chicken. Bake 30 minutes or until chicken is no longer pink.
- Stir sauce. Serve with chicken.

MAKES 4 MAIN-DISH SERVINGS	PREP TIME: 5 MINUTES COOK TIME: 60 MINUTES

TOMATO SOUP-SPICE CAKE

2 cups all-purpose flour
1⅓ cups sugar
4 teaspoons baking powder
1½ teaspoons ground allspice
1 teaspoon baking soda
1 teaspoon ground cinnamon
½ teaspoon ground cloves
1 can (10¾ ounces) CAMPBELL'S condensed Tomato Soup
½ cup vegetable shortening
2 eggs
¼ cup water
Cream cheese frosting (optional)

- Preheat oven to 350°F. Grease and flour two 8-inch round cake pans.
- In large bowl, combine flour, sugar, baking powder, allspice, baking soda, cinnamon, cloves, soup, shortening, eggs and water. With mixer at low speed, beat until well mixed, constantly scraping bowl with rubber spatula. At high speed, beat 4 minutes, occasionally scraping bowl. Pour batter into prepared pans.
- Bake 35 to 40 minutes or until toothpick inserted in center comes out clean. Cool in pans on wire racks 10 minutes. Carefully remove from pans; cool completely. Frost with cream cheese frosting. If desired, garnish with *fresh mint* and *orange slices.*

MAKES 8 SERVINGS	PREP TIME: 10 MINUTES
	BAKE & COOL TIME: 3 HOURS

Resource- ful Americans have always made the most of the foods available to them. This moist spice cake was first made with canned toma- toes, but the toma- toes were replaced by condensed toma- to soup in the 1920s. Since then, this basic recipe has changed very little, but it has been transformed into a fruitcake, pineapple upside-down cake and a microwave cake.

1993
ADVERTISEMENT

SAVORY POT ROAST

 2 tablespoons vegetable oil
3½- to 4-pound boneless beef bottom round *or* chuck pot roast
 1 can (10¾ ounces) CAMPBELL'S condensed
     Cream of Mushroom *or* 1 can (11⅛ ounces) Italian Tomato Soup
 1 pouch CAMPBELL'S Dry Onion Soup and Recipe Mix
1¼ cups water
 6 medium potatoes (about 2 pounds), peeled and quartered
     (about 5½ cups)
 6 medium carrots (about 1 pound), cut into 2-inch pieces
     (about 3 cups)
 2 tablespoons all-purpose flour

- In 6-quart Dutch oven over medium-high heat, in hot oil, cook roast until browned on all sides. Remove; set aside. Pour off fat.
- In same Dutch oven, combine mushroom soup, onion soup mix and *1 cup* of water. Heat to boiling. Return roast to Dutch oven. Reduce heat to low. Cover; cook 2 hours, turning roast occasionally.
- Add potatoes and carrots. Cover; cook 40 minutes more or until roast and vegetables are fork-tender, stirring occasionally.
- Transfer roast and vegetables to platter. Cut roast across the grain. Cover and keep warm while preparing sauce.
- In cup, stir together flour and remaining ¼ *cup* water until smooth. Gradually stir into sauce in Dutch oven. Over medium heat, cook until mixture boils and thickens, stirring constantly. Serve sauce with roast; pass remaining sauce. If desired, garnish with *fresh caraway*.

MAKES 8 MAIN-DISH SERVINGS	PREP TIME: 5 MINUTES COOK TIME: 3 HOURS

BASIL-CHICKEN PARMESAN

> 2 tablespoons all-purpose flour
> 1½ teaspoons dried basil leaves, crushed
> 4 skinless, boneless chicken breast halves (about 1 pound)
> 1 tablespoon olive oil
> 1 can (10¾ ounces) CAMPBELL'S HEALTHY REQUEST condensed Tomato Soup
> 2 tablespoons Chablis *or* other dry white wine
> 2 tablespoons water
> ¼ cup finely chopped green pepper
> 2 tablespoons grated Parmesan cheese
> 2 cups hot cooked rice

- On waxed paper, combine flour and *1 teaspoon* basil. Lightly coat chicken with flour mixture.
- In 10-inch skillet over medium-high heat, in hot oil, cook chicken 10 minutes or until browned on both sides. Remove; set aside. Pour off fat.
- In same skillet, combine soup, wine, water and remaining *½ teaspoon* basil. Heat to boiling. Return chicken to skillet. Reduce heat to low. Cover; cook 5 minutes or until chicken is no longer pink, stirring occasionally. Sprinkle with green pepper and cheese. Serve with rice.

MAKES 4 MAIN-DISH SERVINGS	PREP TIME: 10 MINUTES COOK TIME: 20 MINUTES

BROTH-SIMMERED RICE

> 1 can (14½ ounces) SWANSON Ready To Serve Clear Vegetable, Chicken *or* Beef Broth
> ¾ cup uncooked regular long-grain rice

- In 2-quart saucepan over medium-high heat, heat broth to boiling. Stir in rice. Reduce heat to low. Cover; cook 20 minutes or until rice is tender and broth is absorbed.

MAKES ABOUT 2 CUPS OR 4 SIDE-DISH SERVINGS	PREP TIME: 5 MINUTES COOK TIME: 25 MINUTES

BROCCOLI-BEEF STIR-FRY

1 **pound boneless beef sirloin *or* top round steak,**
 ¾ **inch thick**
2 **tablespoons vegetable oil**
2 **cups fresh broccoli flowerets**
½ **teaspoon ground ginger**
¼ **teaspoon garlic powder *or* 2 cloves garlic, minced**
1 **can (10¾ ounces) CAMPBELL'S condensed Tomato Soup**
2 **tablespoons soy sauce**
1 **tablespoon vinegar**
4 **cups hot cooked rice**

- Slice beef across the grain into thin strips.
- In 10-inch skillet or wok over medium-high heat, in *1 tablespoon* hot oil, stir-fry *half* of the beef until browned. Remove; set aside. Repeat with remaining beef.
- Reduce heat to medium. In same skillet, in remaining *1 tablespoon* hot oil, stir-fry broccoli, ginger and garlic powder until broccoli is tender-crisp.
- Stir in soup, soy sauce and vinegar. Heat to boiling. Return beef to skillet. Heat through, stirring occasionally. Serve over rice.

Makes About 3 Cups or 4 Main-Dish Servings	Prep Time: 10 Minutes Cook Time: 20 Minutes

Although broccoli has been popular since the 1920s, it has been used as a food since the time of the ancient Romans. Because good, fresh broccoli is now so easy to find, many ways of preparing it have been developed to make the most of its freshness. One of these is stir-frying.

1934
ADVERTISEMENT

CHICKEN VEGETABLE STIR-FRY

2 tablespoons cornstarch
1 can (14½ ounces) SWANSON Ready To Serve Clear Vegetable *or*
    Chicken Broth
1 tablespoon soy sauce
¼ teaspoon ground ginger
2 tablespoons vegetable oil
1 pound skinless, boneless chicken breasts, cut into strips
5 cups cut-up fresh vegetables (broccoli, mushrooms, carrots,
    celery and green onions)
⅛ teaspoon garlic powder *or* 1 clove garlic, minced
2 recipes Broth-Simmered Rice (see recipe, page 24) *or* 4 cups
    hot cooked rice

- In small bowl, stir together cornstarch, broth, soy sauce and ginger until smooth; set aside.
- In 10-inch skillet or wok over medium-high heat, in *1 tablespoon* hot oil, stir-fry *half* of the chicken until browned. Remove; set aside. Repeat with remaining chicken.
- Reduce heat to medium. In same skillet, in remaining *1 tablespoon* hot oil, stir-fry vegetables and garlic until vegetables are tender-crisp.
- Add reserved cornstarch mixture. Cook until mixture boils and thickens, stirring constantly. Return chicken to skillet. Heat through, stirring occasionally. Serve over rice. If desired, garnish with *fresh chives.*

MAKES ABOUT 5 CUPS OR 4 MAIN-DISH SERVINGS	PREP TIME: 20 MINUTES COOK TIME: 20 MINUTES

1992
ADVERTISEMENT

LEMON-BROCCOLI CHICKEN

1 lemon
1 tablespoon vegetable oil
4 skinless, boneless chicken breast halves (about 1 pound)
1 can (10¾ ounces) CAMPBELL'S condensed Cream of Broccoli Soup
¼ cup milk
⅛ teaspoon pepper

- Cut 4 thin slices from lemon; set aside. Squeeze *2 teaspoons* juice from remaining lemon; set aside.
- In 10-inch skillet over medium-high heat, in hot oil, cook chicken 10 minutes or until browned on both sides. Remove; set aside. Pour off fat.
- In same skillet, combine soup, milk, reserved lemon juice and pepper. Heat to boiling. Return chicken to skillet.
- Reduce heat to low. Cover; cook 5 minutes or until chicken is no longer pink, stirring occasionally. If desired, serve with *parsley buttered orzo;* garnish with reserved lemon slices and *fresh sage.*

MAKES 4 MAIN-DISH SERVINGS	PREP TIME: 5 MINUTES COOK TIME: 20 MINUTES

1927
ADVERTISEMENT

SOUPER CHICKEN TETRAZZINI

1 **can (10¾ ounces) CAMPBELL'S condensed Cream of Mushroom Soup**
½ **cup milk**
1 **small onion, finely chopped (about ¼ cup)**
¼ **cup grated Parmesan cheese**
¼ **cup sour cream**
1½ **cups cubed cooked chicken *or* turkey**
1 **small zucchini, cut in half lengthwise and thinly sliced (about 1 cup)**
1½ **cups cooked spaghetti (3 ounces dry)**

- In large bowl, combine soup, milk, onion, cheese and sour cream. Stir in chicken and zucchini. Add spaghetti; toss gently to coat. Spoon into 1½-quart casserole.
- Bake at 375°F. for 30 minutes or until hot and bubbling. Serve with *additional cheese.*

MAKES ABOUT 4 CUPS OR 4 MAIN-DISH SERVINGS	PREP TIME: 20 MINUTES COOK TIME: 30 MINUTES

BAKED ONION CHICKEN

1 **pouch CAMPBELL'S Dry Onion Soup Mix with Chicken Broth**
⅔ **cup dry bread crumbs**
⅛ **teaspoon pepper**
1 **egg *or* 2 egg whites**
2 **tablespoons water**
12 **skinless, boneless chicken thighs *or* 6 skinless, boneless chicken breast halves (about 1½ pounds)**
2 **tablespoons margarine *or* butter, melted (optional)**

- With rolling pin, crush soup mix in pouch. On waxed paper, combine soup mix, bread crumbs and pepper.
- In shallow dish, beat together egg and water. Dip chicken into egg mixture; coat with crumb mixture.
- On baking sheet, arrange chicken. Drizzle with margarine. Bake at 400°F. for 20 minutes or until chicken is no longer pink.

MAKES 6 MAIN-DISH SERVINGS	PREP TIME: 10 MINUTES COOK TIME: 20 MINUTES

CRISPY CHICKEN WITH ASPARAGUS SAUCE

1 **egg** *or* **2 egg whites**
4 **skinless, boneless chicken breast halves** *or* **8 boneless chicken thighs**
  (about 1 pound)
½ **cup dry bread crumbs**
2 **tablespoons vegetable oil**
1 **can (10¾ ounces) CAMPBELL'S condensed Cream of Asparagus Soup**
⅓ **cup water**
⅓ **cup milk**
  Grated Parmesan cheese
4 **cups hot cooked rice**

- In shallow dish, beat egg. Dip chicken into egg. On waxed paper, coat chicken with bread crumbs.
- In 10-inch skillet over medium-low heat, in hot oil, cook chicken 15 minutes or until browned on both sides and no longer pink. Remove; keep warm. Pour off fat.
- In same skillet, combine soup, water and milk. Heat through, stirring occasionally. Spoon soup mixture over chicken. Sprinkle with cheese. Serve with rice.

Makes 4 Main-Dish Servings	Prep Time: 10 Minutes Cook Time: 20 Minutes

SINCE THE FIRST CAMPBELL COOKBOOK, "HELPS FOR THE HOSTESS" WAS PUBLISHED IN 1916, CAMPBELL COOKBOOKS HAVE BEEN A KIND OF "FAMILY ALBUM" OF AMERICAN TASTES, TRENDS AND LIFESTYLES.

BROCCOLI-CHEESE CHICKEN

1 tablespoon margarine *or* butter
4 skinless, boneless chicken breast halves (about 1 pound)
1 can (10¾ ounces) CAMPBELL'S condensed Broccoli Cheese Soup
2 cups fresh broccoli flowerets
⅓ cup water *or* milk
⅛ teaspoon pepper

- In 10-inch skillet over medium-high heat, in hot margarine, cook chicken 10 minutes or until browned on both sides. Remove; set aside.
- In same skillet, combine soup, broccoli, water and pepper. Heat to boiling. Return chicken to skillet. Reduce heat to low. Cover; cook 10 minutes or until chicken is no longer pink and broccoli is tender, stirring occasionally. If desired, garnish with *plum slices.*

MAKES 4 MAIN-DISH SERVINGS	PREP TIME: 5 MINUTES COOK TIME: 25 MINUTES

CHICKEN-BROCCOLI DIVAN

1 pound fresh broccoli, cut into flowerets (about 4 cups), cooked and drained
1½ cups cubed cooked chicken
1 can (10¾ ounces) CAMPBELL'S condensed Broccoli Cheese Soup
⅓ cup milk
½ cup shredded Cheddar cheese, optional
2 tablespoons dry bread crumbs
1 tablespoon margarine *or* butter, melted

- In 9-inch pie plate or 2-quart oblong baking dish, arrange broccoli and chicken. In bowl, combine soup and milk; pour over broccoli and chicken.
- Sprinkle cheese over soup mixture. In cup, combine bread crumbs and margarine; sprinkle over cheese.
- Bake at 450°F. for 20 minutes or until hot and bubbling.

MAKES 4 MAIN-DISH SERVINGS	PREP TIME: 15 MINUTES COOK TIME: 20 MINUTES

The combination of tortilla chips, cheese and chilies first became popular in Mexican restaurants whose customers soon realized that Nachos could be made easily at home. A native Mexican cook would use leftover tortillas, cut them into bite-size pieces and fry them until crisp. Today, Nachos enjoy a position at the halftime snack table as a home team favorite.

CALIFORNIA ONION DIP

1 **pouch CAMPBELL'S Dry Onion Soup Mix with Chicken Broth**
1 **container (16 ounces) sour cream**
   Assorted fresh vegetables

- In medium bowl, combine soup mix and sour cream. Cover; refrigerate 2 hours before serving.
- Serve with fresh vegetables for dipping. If desired, garnish with *fresh marjoram.*

MAKES ABOUT 2 CUPS	PREP TIME: 5 MINUTES
	CHILL TIME: 2 HOURS

NACHOS

1 **can (10¾ ounces) CAMPBELL'S condensed Cheddar Cheese Soup**
½ **cup salsa**
1 **bag (about 10 ounces) tortilla chips**
   VLASIC *or* EARLY CALIFORNIA sliced pitted Ripe Olives,
      sliced green onions *and/or* chopped green or sweet red pepper

- In 1½-quart saucepan, combine soup and salsa. Over low heat, heat through, stirring often.
- Arrange tortilla chips evenly on serving platter. Spoon sauce over chips. Top with olives, onions and/or chopped pepper.

MAKES ABOUT 1½ CUPS	PREP TIME: 10 MINUTES
SAUCE OR 6 SERVINGS	COOK TIME: 5 MINUTES

CALIFORNIA ONION DIP (*top*),
NACHOS (*bottom*)

SAVORY CHICKEN AND MUSHROOMS

> 2 tablespoons margarine *or* butter
> 4 skinless, boneless chicken breast halves (about 1 pound)
> 1½ cups fresh broccoli flowerets
> 1½ cups sliced fresh mushrooms (about 4 ounces)
> 1 can (10¾ ounces) CAMPBELL'S condensed
>   Cream of Chicken & Broccoli Soup
> ¼ cup milk
> 2 tablespoons Dijon-style mustard
> 4 cups hot cooked egg noodles (about 4 cups dry)

- In 10-inch skillet over medium-high heat, in *1 tablespoon* hot margarine, cook chicken 10 minutes or until browned on both sides. Remove; set aside.
- Reduce heat to medium. In same skillet, in remaining *1 tablespoon* hot margarine, cook broccoli and mushrooms until vegetables are tender and liquid is evaporated, stirring often.
- Stir in soup, milk and mustard. Heat to boiling. Return chicken to skillet. Reduce heat to low. Cover; cook 5 minutes or until chicken is no longer pink, stirring occasionally. Serve with noodles. If desired, garnish with *carrot curls* and *fresh parsley.*

MAKES 4 MAIN-DISH SERVINGS	PREP TIME: 15 MINUTES
	COOK TIME: 25 MINUTES

SKILLET MAC 'N' BEEF

1 **pound ground beef**
1 **medium onion, chopped (about ½ cup)**
1 **can (10¾ ounces) CAMPBELL'S condensed Cream of Celery Soup**
¼ **cup ketchup**
1 **tablespoon Worcestershire sauce**
2 **cups cooked corkscrew macaroni (about 1½ cups dry)**

- In 10-inch skillet over medium-high heat, cook beef and onion until beef is browned and onion is tender, stirring to separate meat. Spoon off fat.
- Stir in soup, ketchup and Worcestershire sauce; add macaroni. Reduce heat to low. Heat through, stirring occasionally.

MAKES ABOUT 4½ CUPS OR 4 MAIN-DISH SERVINGS	PREP TIME: 10 MINUTES COOK TIME: 15 MINUTES

CHEDDAR POTATO SLICES

1 **can (10¾ ounces) CAMPBELL'S condensed**
  Cream of Mushroom Soup
½ **teaspoon paprika**
½ **teaspoon pepper**
4 **medium baking potatoes (about 1¼ pounds), cut into**
  ¼-inch slices (about 4 cups)
1 **cup shredded Cheddar cheese (4 ounces)**

- In small bowl, combine soup, paprika and pepper.
- In greased 2-quart oblong baking dish, arrange potatoes in overlapping rows. Sprinkle with cheese; spoon soup mixture over cheese.
- Cover with foil. Bake at 400°F. for 45 minutes. Uncover; bake 10 minutes more or until potatoes are fork-tender.

MAKES ABOUT 5 CUPS OR 6 SIDE-DISH SERVINGS	PREP TIME: 15 MINUTES COOK TIME: 55 MINUTES

*P*otatoes have been cooked in just about every way imaginable and some people even prefer them raw. The infamous bank robber, John Dillinger, used a potato to escape from prison—he carved it in the shape of a gun and dyed it with iodine. Now that's American ingenuity!

CREAMY VEGETABLE MEDLEY

1 can (10¾ ounces) CAMPBELL'S condensed Golden Corn
      or Cheddar Cheese Soup
½ cup milk
2 cups fresh broccoli flowerets
2 medium carrots, sliced (about 1 cup)
1 cup fresh cauliflowerets
⅓ cup diced sweet red *or* green pepper, optional
½ cup shredded Cheddar cheese (2 ounces), optional
1 tablespoon chopped fresh cilantro
½ to 1 teaspoon Louisiana-style hot sauce, optional

- In 2-quart saucepan, combine soup and milk. Over medium heat, heat to boiling, stirring occasionally.
- Add vegetables. Reduce heat to low. Cover; cook 15 minutes or until vegetables are tender, stirring occasionally.
- Stir in cheese, cilantro and hot sauce.
- Heat until cheese is melted. If desired, garnish with *fresh cilantro.*

MAKES ABOUT 3½ CUPS OR 6 SIDE-DISH SERVINGS	PREP TIME: 15 MINUTES COOK TIME: 20 MINUTES

BROCCOLI-CHEESE POTATO TOPPER

1 can (10¾ ounces) CAMPBELL'S condensed Cheddar Cheese Soup
2 tablespoons sour cream *or* plain yogurt
½ teaspoon Dijon-style mustard
1 cup cooked broccoli flowerets
4 hot baked potatoes, split

- In 1½-quart saucepan, combine soup, sour cream and mustard; add broccoli. Over medium heat, heat through, stirring occasionally.
  Serve over potatoes. If desired, garnish with *cherry tomatoes* and *fresh basil.*

MAKES ABOUT 1½ CUPS OR 4 SIDE-DISH SERVINGS	PREP TIME: 10 MINUTES COOK TIME: 10 MINUTES

Campbell's test kitchens are always looking for new ways to update time-tested favorite recipes as well as develop exciting new dishes that reflect the tastes, trends and demands of your lifestyle. But the most important kitchen, by far, is your own—where you and your family are the final authority on good taste.

Americans love good food and thrive on competition. Over the years, Campbell's Cooking With Soup recipe contests have been a spirited and special way of putting the two together and placing Americans' creativity squarely on the front burner. Many of these prize-winning recipes are part of new trends or have become classics in their own right.

Here are some of the latest prize-winning recipes, all made quick, easy

FESTIVE CHICKEN

1 teaspoon onion powder
½ teaspoon paprika
¼ teaspoon garlic powder
¼ teaspoon pepper
2 pounds chicken parts, skinned
1 can (10¾ ounces) CAMPBELL'S condensed
    Cream of Mushroom Soup
⅓ cup buttermilk
1 small sweet red pepper, chopped
4 green onions, sliced (about ½ cup)

- In cup, combine first 4 ingredients.
- In 2-quart oblong baking dish, arrange chicken. Sprinkle with seasoning mixture. Bake at 375°F. for 30 minutes.
- Combine soup, buttermilk, red pepper and onions; spoon over chicken. Bake 30 minutes more or until chicken is no longer pink and juices run clear. Stir sauce. If desired, garnish with *fresh parsley.*

MAKES 4 MAIN-DISH SERVINGS	PREP TIME: 10 MINUTES
	COOK TIME: 60 MINUTES

VEGETABLES WITH BROCCOLI-LEMON SAUCE

3 pounds small red potatoes, quartered
2 cups fresh broccoli flowerets
1 large sweet red pepper, cut into rings
1 can (10¾ ounces) CAMPBELL'S condensed Cream of Broccoli Soup
½ cup mayonnaise
4 green onions, finely chopped (about ¼ cup)
1 tablespoon lemon juice
¼ teaspoon dried thyme leaves, crushed

- In 6-quart Dutch oven over high heat, in 1 inch boiling water, cook potatoes 10 minutes.
- Add broccoli and pepper; cook 5 minutes or until tender. Drain in colander.
- In 2-quart saucepan over medium heat, combine soup and remaining ingredients. Heat through, stirring occasionally. Pour over vegetables.

MAKES 8 SIDE-DISH SERVINGS	PREP TIME: 10 MINUTES
	COOK TIME: 20 MINUTES

Approximately 325 million cans of Campbell's Cream of Mushroom Soup are sold each year. About eighty percent is purchased for use in recipes, like Festive Chicken.

WINNING RECIPE FROM
DEAS COBURN,
BURSLY, LA.

Vegetables with Broccoli-Lemon Sauce was the Grand Prize Winner of a "How to Get President Bush to Eat Broccoli" recipe contest in 1991.

WINNING RECIPE FROM
PRISCILLA YEE,
CONCORD, CA.

ITALIAN PEPPER STEAK

1 **pound boneless beef sirloin *or* top round steak, ¾ inch thick**
2 **tablespoons olive *or* vegetable oil**
2 **cups sweet pepper strips (green, red *and/or* orange)**
1 **medium onion, sliced and separated into rings (about ½ cup)**
1 **teaspoon dried oregano leaves, crushed**
¼ **teaspoon garlic powder *or* 2 cloves garlic, minced**
¼ **teaspoon pepper**
1 **can (11⅛ ounces) CAMPBELL'S condensed Italian Tomato Soup**
½ **cup water**
4 **cups hot cooked fusilli *or* spaghetti**

- Slice beef across the grain into thin strips.
- In 10-inch skillet over medium-high heat, in *1 tablespoon* hot oil, cook *half* of the beef until browned, stirring often. Remove; set aside. Repeat with remaining beef.
- Reduce heat to medium. In same skillet, in remaining *1 tablespoon* hot oil, cook sweet peppers, onion, oregano, garlic powder and pepper until vegetables are tender, stirring often.
- Stir in soup and water. Heat to boiling. Return beef to skillet. Heat through, stirring occasionally. Serve over fusilli. If desired, serve with *garlic bread*.

MAKES 4 MAIN-DISH SERVINGS	PREP TIME: 15 MINUTES COOK TIME: 25 MINUTES

FAST AND FABULOUS GOLDEN DIVAN

1¼ cups water
 1 medium onion, chopped (about ½ cup)
 ¼ cup margarine *or* butter
 1 package (8 ounces) PEPPERIDGE FARM Herb Seasoned Stuffing
     (about 4 cups)
 2 cups cooked broccoli cuts
 2 cups cubed cooked turkey *or* chicken
 1 can (10¾ ounces) CAMPBELL'S condensed Golden Corn Soup
 1 cup shredded Cheddar cheese (4 ounces)
 ½ cup milk
 1 can (about 4 ounces) sliced mushrooms, drained (optional)

• In 2-quart saucepan over high heat, heat water, onion and margarine to
  boiling. Remove from heat. Add stuffing; toss to mix well. Spoon into 2-quart
  oblong baking dish. Arrange broccoli and turkey over stuffing.
• In medium bowl, combine soup, ½ *cup* cheese, milk and mushrooms.
  Pour over broccoli and turkey. Sprinkle remaining ½ *cup* cheese over
  soup mixture.
• Bake at 350°F. for 30 minutes or until hot and bubbling. If desired,
  serve with *cucumber-tomato salad;* garnish with *fresh sage* and *thyme.*

MAKES ABOUT 7½ CUPS OR 6 MAIN-DISH SERVINGS	PREP TIME: 15 MINUTES COOK TIME: 35 MINUTES

HEARTY CHICKEN AND SAUSAGE SOUP

½ **pound sweet Italian sausage, casing removed**
2 **cans (14½ ounces *each*) SWANSON Ready To Serve Clear Vegetable Broth**
1 **can (8 ounces) tomato sauce**
1 **large onion, chopped (about 1 cup)**
1 **large carrot, diced (about ⅔ cup)**
1 **rib celery, diced (about ½ cup)**
1 **teaspoon dried oregano leaves, crushed**
½ **teaspoon garlic powder *or* 4 cloves garlic, minced**
⅛ **teaspoon pepper**
1½ **cups cooked medium shell macaroni (about 1 cup dry)**
1 **cup diced cooked chicken**

- In 3-quart saucepan over medium-high heat, cook sausage until browned, stirring to separate meat. Spoon off fat.
- Add broth, tomato sauce, onion, carrot, celery, oregano, garlic powder and pepper. Cover; heat to boiling. Reduce heat to low. Cook 20 minutes or until vegetables are tender, stirring occasionally.
- Add macaroni and chicken. Heat through, stirring occasionally.

MAKES ABOUT 7 CUPS OR 4 MAIN-DISH SERVINGS	PREP TIME: 15 MINUTES COOK TIME: 40 MINUTES

CALCUTTA CURRY

2 tablespoons vegetable oil
1 pound skinless, boneless chicken breasts, cut into 1-inch cubes
1 medium sweet red pepper, cut into strips (about 1 cup)
1½ teaspoons curry powder
¼ teaspoon ground ginger *or* grated fresh ginger
¼ to ½ teaspoon crushed red pepper
⅛ teaspoon garlic powder
1 can (10¾ ounces) CAMPBELL'S condensed Cream of Asparagus Soup
⅔ cup milk
2 tablespoons chopped fresh cilantro *or* parsley
4 cups hot cooked rice
¼ cup flaked coconut
¼ cup chopped peanuts

- In 10-inch skillet over medium-high heat, in *1 tablespoon* hot oil, cook *half* of the chicken until browned, stirring often. Remove; set aside. Repeat with remaining chicken.
- Reduce heat to medium. In same skillet, in remaining *1 tablespoon* hot oil, cook sweet red pepper, curry powder, ginger, crushed red pepper and garlic powder until sweet red pepper is tender-crisp, stirring often.
- Stir in soup, milk and *1 tablespoon* cilantro. Heat to boiling. Return chicken to skillet. Reduce heat to low. Cover; cook 5 minutes or until chicken is no longer pink, stirring occasionally. Serve over rice. Sprinkle with remaining *1 tablespoon* cilantro, coconut and peanuts.

Makes 4 Main-Dish Servings	Prep Time: 15 Minutes Cook Time: 25 Minutes

In India, curry powder was prepared as far back as 5,000 years ago, and many Indian cooks still prepare their own blends by mixing up to 20 spices, herbs and seeds, such as cloves, cinnamon, ginger, chilies, turmeric, coriander, cumin and fennel seed. In America, commercially-prepared curry powder is most commonly purchased by consumers.

WINNING RECIPE FROM LOIS ROSEN, LOS ANGELES, CA.

*M*odern
legend has it that
Cubby Broccoli,
producer of the
James Bond-007
movies, is a mem-
ber of the Italian
agricultural family
that brought broc-
coli to the vegetable
forefront in the ear-
ly part of this centu-
ry. Whether it's fact
or fiction, or a little
bit of both, broccoli
is no "secret agent"
in Campbell's
Broccoli Cheese
Soup. This popular
soup is a combina-
tion of broccoli flow-
erets in a real
Cheddar cheese
soup base, ideal for
use as a soup or as
an ingredient in
recipes like South-of-
the-Border Chicken.

WINNING RECIPE FROM
BONNIE MORGAN,
SACRAMENTO, CA.

SOUTH-OF-THE-BORDER CHICKEN

1 tablespoon margarine *or* butter
4 skinless, boneless chicken breast halves (about 1 pound)
1 can (10¾ ounces) CAMPBELL'S condensed Broccoli Cheese Soup
⅓ cup milk
4 cups hot cooked rice
1 small avocado, sliced (optional)
   Salsa
   Sour cream

- In 10-inch skillet over medium-high heat, in hot margarine, cook chicken 10 minutes or until browned on both sides. Remove; set aside.
- In same skillet, combine soup and milk. Heat to boiling. Return chicken to skillet. Reduce heat to low. Cover; cook 5 minutes or until chicken is no longer pink, stirring occasionally.
- Serve over rice with avocado. Top with salsa and sour cream. If desired, garnish with *fresh cilantro* and *fresh chili pepper*. Pass tortilla chips, if desired.

MAKES 4 MAIN-DISH SERVINGS	PREP TIME: 5 MINUTES COOK TIME: 20 MINUTES

THE ENGINE BEHIND V8 JUICE

Even during the Great Depression, Americans were health-conscious. In response to the growing trend, a Mr. W.G. Peacock, Sr., of Evanston, Illinois developed the idea of packaging and selling many kinds of vegetable juices—carrot juice, spinach juice, lettuce juice and celery juice and even watercress juice. However, customers found their taste so unappealing that they tried them once and never again!

Peacock and his son then combined each of the separate juices into one juice, which they named "Veg-min." A store clerk suggested changing the name of the new, delicious beverage to V-8, after the V-8 engine, and the nutritious thirst quencher soon became widely popular in the midwest. Campbell Soup Company acquired the *V8-brand* Vegetable Juice in 1948 and began distributing it nationally.

If the name and face from this 1951 "V8" ad don't ring a bell, think of the two fingers he's holding up as the number of terms he spent in office as President!

Today, *V8* 100% Vegetable Juice is available in Original, Low Sodium, Light 'n Tangy, Spicy Hot and Picante varieties. And, as you'll see in these serving ideas, the tasty blend of eight vegetable juices is a great enhancer for appetizers, entrées, side dishes, sauces and non-alcoholic beverages. A 6-ounce glass of *V8* Juice also provides a serving of vegetables.

LIGHT 'N TANGY TWISTER

2 cups LIGHT 'N TANGY V8 Vegetable Juice *or* V8 Vegetable Juice
⅓ cup orange juice
¼ cup grapefruit juice
2 teaspoons honey

- In pitcher, combine "V8" juice, orange juice, grapefruit juice and honey.
- Pour over ice. If desired, garnish with *celery rib.*

Makes About 2½ Cups or 3 Servings	Prep Time: 5 Minutes

SPICY HOT REFRESHER

1½ cups SPICY HOT V8 Vegetable Juice
½ cup chopped, seeded, peeled cucumber
1 tablespoon lime juice
¼ teaspoon chili powder
1 cup ice cubes

- In covered blender or food processor, combine "V8" juice, cucumber, lime juice and chili powder. Blend until smooth. Add ice cubes, one at a time, blending until ice is finely crushed.
- Serve immediately.

Makes About 2½ Cups or 4 Servings	Prep Time: 10 Minutes

Non-alcoholic drinks are becoming more and more popular as folks all across the country realize their many benefits. Since there is a wide variety of these beverages, ranging from spicy warmers to crushed ice refreshers, there is no need to sacrifice festivity when refraining from alcohol. Enjoy!

TANGY BROILED CHICKEN

6 skinless, boneless chicken breast halves (about 1½ pounds)
1 cup refrigerated MARIE'S ZESTY Fat Free Red Wine Vinaigrette
¾ cup LIGHT 'N TANGY V8 Vegetable Juice *or*
    V8 PICANTE Vegetable Juice
1 tablespoon cornstarch

- Place large plastic bag in deep bowl; add chicken. In 2-cup measure, combine vinaigrette and "V8" juice; pour over chicken. Close bag.
- Refrigerate at least 4 hours or overnight, turning chicken occasionally. Remove chicken from marinade and arrange on rack in broiler pan. Reserve marinade.
- In 1-quart saucepan, stir together cornstarch and reserved marinade until smooth. Over medium heat, cook until sauce boils and thickens, stirring constantly.
- Brush chicken with sauce. Broil 4 inches from heat 15 minutes or until chicken is no longer pink, turning once and brushing often with sauce during cooking. If desired, serve with *orange-onion salad* and *parslied noodles.*

Makes 6 Main-Dish Servings	Marinating Time: 4 Hours
	Prep Time: 5 Minutes
	Cook Time: 20 Minutes

BLOODY EIGHT

3 cups V8 Vegetable Juice
1 teaspoon prepared horseradish
1 teaspoon Worcestershire sauce
½ teaspoon hot pepper sauce

- In pitcher, combine "V8" juice, horseradish, Worcestershire sauce and hot pepper sauce.
- Pour over ice. If desired, garnish with *celery stick.*

Makes About 3 Cups or 4 Servings	Prep Time: 5 Minutes

The Bloody Eight is a non-alcoholic version of the classic Bloody Mary, a refreshing beverage with a hearty, spicy tang made from tomato or vegetable juice and vodka.

TANGY BROILED CHICKEN (*bottom*),
BLOODY EIGHT (*top*)

Fiesta Rice

1 tablespoon vegetable oil
1 small green pepper, chopped (about ½ cup)
1 small onion, chopped (about ¼ cup)
3 cups V8 PICANTE Vegetable Juice
¼ teaspoon garlic powder
1 cup uncooked regular long-grain rice
½ cup shredded Monterey Jack cheese (2 ounces)

- In 2-quart saucepan over medium heat, in hot oil, cook pepper and onion until tender, stirring often.
- Add "V8" juice and garlic powder. Heat to boiling. Stir in rice. Reduce heat to low. Cover; cook 15 minutes. Uncover; cook 5 minutes more or until rice is tender and liquid is absorbed, stirring occasionally. Stir in cheese. If desired, garnish with *celery leaves.*

Makes About 4 Cups or 4 Side-Dish Servings	Prep Time: 10 Minutes Cook Time: 30 Minutes

Orange-Mustard Sauce

1 cup V8 Vegetable Juice
½ cup orange marmalade
1 tablespoon Dijon-style mustard

- In 1½-quart saucepan, combine "V8" juice, marmalade and mustard. Over medium-high heat, heat to boiling. Reduce heat to low; cook 10 minutes or until sauce thickens, stirring often.
- Use sauce to baste chicken, pork chops or turkey cutlets during the last few minutes of broiling or grilling.

Makes About 1 Cup Sauce	Prep Time: 5 Minutes Cook Time: 15 Minutes

"Truly it has become the cup that cheers, revives and revivifies," read a 1931 advertisement featuring *Campbell's* Tomato Juice.

The popular comedy team of George Burns and Gracie Allen touted the vitamin-richness of *Campbell's* Tomato Juice in a series of 1935 magazine ads, as well as on their weekly CBS radio program.

Over the years, *Campbell's* Tomato Juice has become so much more than a delicious and refreshing beverage. Its savory, full flavor makes it a terrific starting point for sauces, dips, baked goods and beverages, as well as main courses. Taste for yourself with these zesty recipes.

SHRIMP CREOLE

- **2 tablespoons margarine *or* butter**
- **1 large green pepper, diced (about 1 cup)**
- **2 ribs celery, thinly sliced (about 1 cup)**
- **1 medium onion, chopped (about ½ cup)**
- **½ teaspoon dried oregano leaves, crushed**
- **¼ teaspoon garlic powder *or* 2 cloves garlic, minced**
- **⅛ teaspoon ground red pepper (cayenne)**
- **1½ cups CAMPBELL'S Tomato Juice**
- **1 tablespoon cornstarch**
- **1 pound large shrimp, shelled and deveined**
- **4 cups hot cooked parslied rice**

- In 10-inch skillet over medium heat, in hot margarine, cook green pepper, celery, onion, oregano, garlic powder and red pepper until vegetables are tender-crisp, stirring often.
- Add *1 cup* tomato juice. Heat to boiling. Reduce heat to low. Cover; cook 5 minutes, stirring occasionally.
- Meanwhile, in small bowl, stir together cornstarch and remaining *½ cup* tomato juice until smooth.
- Increase heat to medium. Add cornstarch mixture and shrimp to vegetable mixture. Cook until mixture boils and thickens and shrimp turn pink and opaque, stirring constantly. Serve over rice.

MAKES ABOUT 4 CUPS OR 4 MAIN-DISH SERVINGS	PREP TIME: 20 MINUTES COOK TIME: 20 MINUTES

The shrimp's name comes from its small size, but shrimp vary greatly in size. The tiniest Alaskan pinks come 180 to the pound, while one single Texas shrimp weighed in at 3 pounds. Most shrimp fall in between, with "medium" shrimp at about 30 per pound. The Gulf Coast produces a great deal of the shrimp we eat in America— and it's also the area where this dish was created.

1935
ADVERTISEMENT

ITALIAN CHICKEN AND PASTA

2 tablespoons olive oil
1 pound skinless, boneless chicken breasts, cut into 1-inch pieces
2 cups sliced fresh mushrooms (about 6 ounces)
1 large onion, diced (about 1 cup)
4 teaspoons cornstarch
2 cups CAMPBELL'S Tomato Juice
¼ teaspoon dried basil leaves, crushed
⅛ teaspoon pepper
2 tablespoons chopped fresh parsley *or* 2 teaspoons dried
     parsley flakes
4 cups hot cooked linguine (about 8 ounces dry)

- In 10-inch skillet over medium-high heat, in *1 tablespoon* hot oil, cook *half* of the chicken until browned, stirring often. Remove; set aside. Repeat with remaining chicken.
- Reduce heat to medium. In same skillet, in remaining *1 tablespoon* hot oil, cook mushrooms and onion until vegetables are tender and liquid is evaporated, stirring often.
- In small bowl, stir together cornstarch, tomato juice, basil and pepper until smooth.
- Add cornstarch mixture to vegetable mixture. Cook until mixture boils and thickens, stirring constantly. Return chicken to skillet.Reduce heat to low. Cover; cook 5 minutes or until chicken is no longer pink, stirring occasionally. Stir in parsley.
- Serve over linguine. Sprinkle with additional chopped *fresh parsley.* If desired, serve with *bread sticks;* garnish with *fresh basil* and *fresh sage.*

MAKES ABOUT 4 CUPS OR 4 MAIN-DISH SERVINGS	PREP TIME: 15 MINUTES COOK TIME: 20 MINUTES

1936
ADVERTISEMENT

TWO-BEAN CHILI

1 pound ground beef
1 large green pepper, chopped (about 1 cup)
1 large onion, chopped (about 1 cup)
2 tablespoons chili powder
¼ teaspoon pepper
3 cups CAMPBELL'S Tomato Juice
1 can (about 15 ounces) kidney beans, rinsed and drained
1 can (about 15 ounces) great northern beans, rinsed and drained
 Sour cream, sliced green onions *and* shredded Cheddar cheese

- In 6-quart Dutch oven over medium-high heat, cook beef, green pepper, onion, chili powder and pepper until beef is browned and vegetables are tender, stirring to separate meat. Spoon off fat.
- Add tomato juice, kidney beans and great northern beans. Heat to boiling. Reduce heat to low. Cover; cook 20 minutes to blend flavors, stirring occasionally.
- Top with sour cream. Sprinkle with green onions and cheese. If desired, serve with *bread sticks*.

MAKES ABOUT 6 CUPS OR 6 MAIN-DISH SERVINGS	PREP TIME: 10 MINUTES COOK TIME: 35 MINUTES

Mother of Invention

Margaret Rudkin, a Fairfield, Connecticut wife and mother, founded Pepperidge Farm, Incorporated in 1937 when she was unable to find a wholesome loaf of commercial bread on the market. Margaret took matters into her own hands and began producing and selling commercial bread with "home baked quality." In 1955, she expanded *Pepperidge Farm* products to include cookies, too. Since then hundreds of delicious *Pepperidge Farm* products have been developed, each made with the same attention to quality and wholesomeness as when the company was founded. Pepperidge Farm joined the Campbell family in 1961 and Margaret Rudkin continued to serve as Pepperidge Farm's chairman until her death in 1967.

Margaret Rudkin, a Connecticut housewife and mother, founded one of America's largest producers of premium-quality breads and cookies (TOP).

In pursuit of only the finest ingredients for her bread, Margaret Rudkin ordered stone ground whole wheat flour from this mill in Sudbury, MA. (ABOVE).

A collection of Margaret Rudkin's early recipes, circa 1963 (LEFT).

Chicken a la King

1   **package (10 ounces) PEPPERIDGE FARM frozen Puff Pastry Shells**
1   **small green pepper, diced (about ½ cup)**
2   **tablespoons margarine *or* butter**
1   **can (10¾ ounces) CAMPBELL'S condensed Cream of Chicken Soup**
2   **cups cubed, cooked chicken *or* turkey**
½   **cup milk**
¼   **cup diced pimento**

- Bake pastry shells according to package directions.
- In 2-quart saucepan over medium heat, in hot margarine, cook pepper until tender, stirring occasionally. Add soup, chicken, milk and pimento. Heat through, stirring occasionally. Spoon evenly among warm pastry shells.

Makes 6 Main-Dish Servings	Prep Time: 10 Minutes Cook Time: 15 Minutes

Banana Split Cake

24 **PEPPERIDGE FARM Bordeaux Cookies, broken**
2   **medium bananas, thinly sliced**
1   **jar (13 ounces) MARIE'S Creamy Glaze for Bananas**
1   **container (8 ounces) frozen whipped topping, thawed (3 cups)**
    ***or* whipped heavy cream**
2   **tablespoons chocolate syrup**
¼   **cup chopped peanuts**

- In 2-quart casserole, arrange in single layer, *half* of the cookies, *half* of the bananas, *half* of the glaze and *half* of the whipped topping. Repeat layers.
- Drizzle chocolate syrup over topping. Cover; refrigerate at least 4 hours or overnight before serving. Just before serving, sprinkle with peanuts.

Makes 8 Servings	Prep Time: 10 Minutes Chill Time: 4 Hours

Chicken à la King, a favorite choice for luncheon menus, is a great way to use leftover chicken. A comforting nineteenth-century dish, its origins are unknown. Some say the name is a version of Chicken à la Keene, and that it was created in London. Others claim it was first made at the Brighton Beach Hotel in New York and was named for a family in the hotel business named King.

SWEET AND SOUR STUFFED PORK CHOPS

6 boneless pork loin chops, 1½ inches thick (about 3 pounds)
1 can (8 ounces) crushed pineapple, undrained
½ cup water
1 rib celery, chopped (about ½ cup)
4 tablespoons margarine *or* butter
2 tablespoons packed brown sugar
2 tablespoons soy sauce
1 tablespoon cider vinegar
½ teaspoon garlic powder
1 package (8 ounces) PEPPERIDGE FARM Corn Bread Stuffing

- Cut a 4- to 5-inch long slit to make pocket in each pork chop; set aside.
- In 2-quart saucepan over medium heat, combine *undrained* pineapple, water, celery, margarine, brown sugar, soy sauce, vinegar and garlic powder. Heat to boiling, stirring occasionally.
- Add stuffing; toss lightly to coat. Spoon mixture into pork chop pockets. Arrange chops, stuffing-side up in 2-quart oblong baking dish. Cover with foil.
- Bake at 350°F. for 20 minutes. Uncover; bake 25 minutes more or until stuffing is golden brown and chops are no longer pink. If desired, serve with *roasted onions* and *green and sweet yellow pepper strips;* garnish with *fresh sage.*

MAKES 6 MAIN-DISH SERVINGS	PREP TIME: 15 MINUTES
	COOK TIME: 50 MINUTES

APPLE STRUDEL

1 **sheet PEPPERIDGE FARM frozen Puff Pastry**
1 **egg**
1 **teaspoon water**
2 **tablespoons sugar**
1 **tablespoon all-purpose flour**
¼ **teaspoon ground cinnamon**
2 **large cooking apples, peeled, cored and thinly sliced (about 3 cups)**
2 **tablespoons raisins**

- Thaw pastry 20 minutes. In cup, combine egg and water; set aside. Meanwhile, preheat oven to 375°F. Grease 15- by 10-inch jelly-roll pan.
- On lightly floured surface, roll out pastry sheet into a 15- by 12-inch rectangle; place on prepared jelly-roll pan.
- In large bowl, combine sugar, flour and cinnamon. Add apples and raisins; toss to coat well. Arrange apple mixture down one 15-inch side of rectangle to within 1-inch of edge.
- Brush edges of dough with some egg mixture. Roll up pastry, jelly-roll fashion, placing seam-side down on prepared pan. Pinch ends and tuck under. Brush strudel with egg mixture. Cut several 2-inch long diagonal slits, about 2-inches apart, on top of pastry. Bake 35 minutes or until golden.
- Cool in pan on wire rack about 30 minutes before serving. Serve warm. If desired, garnish with *whipped cream, cinnamon sticks* and *fresh mint.*

MAKES 6 SERVINGS	PREP TIME: 30 MINUTES
	COOK TIME: 35 MINUTES

1993
ADVERTISEMENT

*I*T'S IN THERE!

The introduction of *Prego* Spaghetti Sauce sparked a sauce revolution. The kettles at Campbell had been simmering with sauce ideas for some time before a breakthrough sauce technology was developed. The new process enabled Campbell to make a spaghetti sauce with superior color and flavor and a consistency like homemade. *Prego* was heralded as "the sauce with the homemade flavor" that you could not only taste, but also see. In the years that followed, many imitators jumped on the "close to homemade" bandwagon, but few can match the vast *Prego* Spaghetti Sauce line.

When you prepare these mouth-watering recipes with thick and rich *Prego* Spaghetti Sauce, you'll discover why Italian food is just about everyone's favorite cuisine. Buon Apettito!

Homemade taste. It's in there.™
Prego® Extra Chunky.

Basil
Mushrooms
Parsley
Tomato Pieces
Oregano

Mushroom & Green Pepper

NEW & IMPROVED!

NOW!
Bigger Tender-
Crisp Vegetable
Chunks

Prego
100% NATURAL
EXTRA CHUNKY®
SPAGHETTI SAUCE

BIGGER CHUNKS!
Bigger Vegetable Chunks
Make Prego Extra Chunky,®
Extra Good!

Homemade Taste, It's In There!

EXTRA-EASY LASAGNA

¾ **pound ground beef**
3 **cups PREGO Traditional Spaghetti Sauce**
1 **container (15 ounces) ricotta cheese**
2 **cups shredded mozzarella cheese (8 ounces)**
6 *uncooked* **lasagna noodles**
¼ **cup water**

- In 10-inch skillet over medium-high heat, cook beef until browned, stirring to separate meat. Spoon off fat. Add spaghetti sauce; heat through, stirring occasionally.
- In 2-quart oblong baking dish, spread *1½ cups* meat mixture. Top with *3 uncooked* lasagna noodles, *half* of the ricotta cheese and *half* of the mozzarella cheese. Repeat layers. Top with remaining meat mixture.
- Slowly pour water around *inside edges* of baking dish. Cover tightly with foil.
- Bake at 375°F. for 45 minutes. Uncover; bake 10 minutes more. Let stand 10 minutes before serving.

Makes 8 Main-Dish Servings	Prep Time: 10 Minutes
	Cook Time: 65 Minutes
	Stand Time: 10 Minutes

PORK CHOPS ITALIANO

1 **tablespoon vegetable oil**
6 **pork chops, each ½ inch thick (about 1½ pounds)**
2 **cups PREGO EXTRA CHUNKY Mushroom & Green Pepper Spaghetti Sauce**
6 **cups hot cooked rice**

- In 10-inch skillet over medium-high heat, in hot oil, cook *half* of the chops 5 minutes or until browned on both sides. Remove; set aside. Repeat with remaining chops. Pour off fat.
- In same skillet, heat spaghetti sauce to boiling. Return chops to skillet. Reduce heat to low. Cover; cook 5 minutes or until chops are no longer pink, stirring occasionally. Serve with rice.

Makes 6 Main-Dish Servings	Prep Time: 5 Minutes
	Cook Time: 20 Minutes

There are many ways to prepare lasagna, but this is the way Americans prefer it—with layers of lasagna noodles, meat sauce and ricotta and mozzarella cheeses. Lasagna is a great main dish to serve when entertaining. It can be made ahead, refrigerated or frozen, and reheated before serving. In this easy recipe, there's no need to precook the noodles—they cook while baking in the oven!

DEEP-DISH PIZZA

1 package (10 ounces) refrigerated pizza crust dough
¾ cup PREGO Pizza Sauce with Pepperoni Chunks
1½ cups shredded mozzarella cheese (6 ounces)

- Preheat oven to 425°F. Grease 10-inch ovenproof skillet.
- Pat dough onto bottom and 1½ inches up side of skillet; prick dough with fork. Bake 12 minutes or until crust is set and begins to brown. Transfer crust to baking sheet.
- Spread pizza sauce over crust. Sprinkle with cheese. Bake 10 minutes or until cheese is melted and crust is golden. Let stand 5 minutes. If desired, garnish with *fresh oregano.* Cut into wedges.

MAKES 4 MAIN-DISH SERVINGS	PREP TIME: 10 MINUTES COOK TIME: 25 MINUTES STAND TIME: 5 MINUTES

GARDEN PITA PIZZAS

3 whole wheat pita breads (6-inch rounds)
1 tablespoon olive *or* vegetable oil
1½ cups fresh broccoli flowerets
3 medium carrots, thinly sliced (about 1 cup)
1 large green pepper, chopped (about 1 cup)
1 green onion, chopped (about 2 tablespoons)
1 cup PREGO Pizza Sauce with Sliced Mushrooms
1 cup shredded mozzarella cheese (4 ounces)

- Split each pita bread into two flat rounds, making 6 rounds. Place on 2 baking sheets. Bake at 400°F. for 5 minutes or until toasted.
  - In 10-inch skillet over medium heat, in hot oil, stir-fry vegetables until tender-crisp, stirring often. Set aside.
- Spread each round with *2 rounded tablespoons* pizza sauce; top with vegetables and cheese. Bake 5 minutes or until cheese melts.

MAKES 6 PIZZAS OR 6 MAIN-DISH SERVINGS	PREP TIME 15 MINUTES COOK TIME 15 MINUTES

CHICKEN PARMESAN

1 **egg** *or* **2 egg whites**
4 **skinless, boneless chicken breast halves (about 1 pound)**
½ **cup Italian-seasoned dry bread crumbs**
2 **tablespoons margarine** *or* **butter**
2 **cups PREGO Traditional Spaghetti Sauce**
½ **cup shredded mozzarella cheese (2 ounces)**
1 **tablespoon grated Parmesan cheese**
1 **tablespoon chopped fresh parsley** *or* **1 teaspoon dried parsley flakes, optional**
4 **cups hot cooked spaghetti (about 8 ounces dry)**

- In shallow dish, beat egg. Dip chicken into egg. On waxed paper, coat chicken with bread crumbs.
- In 10-inch skillet over medium heat, in hot margarine, cook chicken 10 minutes or until browned on both sides. Remove; set aside.
- In same skillet, heat spaghetti sauce to boiling. Return chicken to skillet. Reduce heat to low. Cover; cook 5 minutes or until chicken is no longer pink, stirring occasionally.
- Sprinkle with mozzarella cheese, Parmesan cheese and parsley. Cover; cook until cheese is melted. Serve with spaghetti and *Italian bread.* If desired, garnish with *fresh herbs.*

MAKES 4 MAIN-DISH SERVINGS	PREP TIME: 5 MINUTES
	COOK TIME: 25 MINUTES

TWO POPULAR PREGO SPAGHETTI SAUCES

M<small>Y</small> F<small>AVORITE</small> Y<small>EAR</small>

The year was 1955. America liked Ike, loved Lucy and was just beginning a lifelong romance with frozen meals in compartmentalized aluminum trays. That spring, Campbell acquired the company that was the innovator of the TV Dinner, C.A. Swanson & Sons. Today, the *Swanson* brand offers a variety of products, from the traditional frozen turkey dinner to delicious canned *Swanson* Premium Chunk Chicken —perfect for great-tasting salads, sandwiches and main dishes.

With *Swanson* Chunk Chicken, you can keep quality, flavorful ready-to-eat chicken right on your kitchen shelf—no stewing, skinning or boning. Taste for yourself with these simple, versatile recipes.

S<small>WANSON</small> TV D<small>INNER</small> P<small>ACKAGE</small>, <small>CIRCA</small> 1955.

Chicken Quesadillas

1 can (10¾ ounces) CAMPBELL'S condensed Cream of Chicken Soup
2 cans (5 ounces *each*) SWANSON Premium Chunk White Chicken, drained
1 cup shredded Cheddar cheese (4 ounces)
1 fresh *or* canned jalapeño pepper, seeded and finely chopped
8 flour tortillas (8 inches *each*)

- Combine soup, chicken, ½ cup cheese and pepper. Top *half* of each tortilla with ¼ *cup* mixture, spread to within ½ inch of edge.
- Moisten edges of tortillas with water; fold over and press to seal. On two baking sheets, arrange tortillas.
- Bake at 400°F. for 8 minutes or until hot. Sprinkle with remaining ½ *cup* cheese. If desired, top with *salsa* and *sour cream.*

Makes 8 Quesadillas or 4 Main-Dish Servings	Prep Time: 15 Minutes Cook Time: 10 Minutes

Easy Chicken Enchiladas

1 can (10 ounces) enchilada sauce
2 cans (5 ounces *each*) SWANSON Premium Chunk White Chicken, drained
1½ cups shredded Cheddar cheese (6 ounces)
1 can (4 ounces) chopped green chilies
1 small onion, chopped (about ¼ cup)
8 corn tortillas (6 inches *each*)

- Spread ½ *can* enchilada sauce in 3-quart oblong baking dish; set aside.
- Combine chicken, *1 cup* cheese, chilies and onion. Along one side of each tortilla, spread about ⅓ *cup* mixture; roll up, jelly-roll fashion. Place seam-side down in dish.
- Pour remaining ½ *can* enchilada sauce over enchiladas. Sprinkle with remaining ½ *cup* cheese. Cover with foil; bake at 350°F. for 25 minutes or until hot. If desired, top with *shredded lettuce, sour cream* and *diced tomato.*

Makes 4 Main-Dish Servings	Prep Time: 20 Minutes Cook Time: 25 Minutes

In the 1990s, Mexican food is hot, hot, hot with consumers! The cuisine of Mexico, which combines Aztec and Mayan Indian traditions with Spanish influences, has been further enhanced by dynamic American-Hispanic influences. The result is an exhilarating hybrid of tastes, textures and varieties that have made such dishes as enchiladas, tacos, tamales and other spicy specialties exciting main meal or side dish foods.

CHINESE CHICKEN SALAD

8 ounces dry spaghetti *or* vermicelli, broken into thirds
⅓ cup water
3 tablespoons creamy peanut butter
2 tablespoons soy sauce
⅛ teaspoon crushed red pepper
1 cup snow peas cut diagonally in 1-inch pieces (about 4 ounces)
2 cans (5 ounces *each*) SWANSON Premium Chunk White Chicken,
      drained
½ cup sweet red pepper strips
3 green onions, sliced (about ⅓ cup)
3 cups shredded spinach leaves (about 4 ounces)

1982
ADVERTISEMENT

- Cook spaghetti according to package directions. Drain in colander.
- Meanwhile, in 1-quart saucepan, combine water, peanut butter, soy sauce and crushed red pepper. Over medium heat, heat to boiling, stirring constantly. Add snow peas; cook until sauce is smooth and peas are tender-crisp, stirring constantly.
- In large bowl, combine hot spaghetti, chicken, red pepper strips and green onions. Pour sauce mixture over spaghetti mixture; toss to coat. Serve immediately on spinach. If desired, garnish with *additional sweet red pepper.*

MAKES ABOUT 6 CUPS OR 6 MAIN-DISH SERVINGS	PREP TIME: 20 MINUTES

CHICKEN SALAD SANDWICHES

1 can (5 ounces) SWANSON Premium Chunk White Chicken, drained
¼ cup chopped celery
3 tablespoons mayonnaise
1 tablespoon finely chopped onion
1 teaspoon lemon juice
   Dash pepper
   Lettuce leaves
   Tomato slices
4 slices bread

- In small bowl, combine chicken, celery, mayonnaise, onion, lemon juice and pepper.
- Arrange lettuce leaves and tomato slices on *2 bread slices.* Top with chicken mixture and remaining *2 bread slices.* If desired, serve with *Vlasic sweet gherkins.*

MAKES 2 MAIN-DISH SERVINGS	PREP TIME: 10 MINUTES

BARBECUED CHICKEN SANDWICHES

1 tablespoon margarine *or* butter
1 small green pepper, chopped (optional)
¼ cup chopped celery
1 small onion, chopped (about ¼ cup)
2 cans (5 ounces *each*) SWANSON Premium Chunk White Chicken, drained
½ cup bottled barbecue sauce
4 hamburger buns, split and toasted

- In 2-quart saucepan over medium heat, in hot margarine, cook green pepper, celery and onion until tender. Add chicken and barbecue sauce. Heat through, stirring occasionally.
- Divide chicken mixture evenly among buns. If desired, serve with *Vlasic cherry peppers* and garnish with *fresh cilantro.*

MAKES 4 MAIN-DISH SERVINGS	PREP TIME: 10 MINUTES
	COOK TIME: 10 MINUTES

CHICKEN SALAD SANDWICHES *(top)*,
BARBECUED CHICKEN SANDWICHES *(bottom)*

DRESSING UP AMERICA

The story behind the early success of *Marie's* Salad Dressings and Glazes might easily be called "Mr. Smith Goes to Washington"—Washington state, that is!

Harold Smith, a cook hailing from Oregon, migrated to neighboring Washington state in the 1950s and took a job at a Seattle-area restaurant known as Marie's Cafe. It was there in the basement of the cafe that he created a blue cheese salad dressing that became a local sensation. By 1964, *Marie's* Blue Cheese Dressing was grossing a million dollars a year in sales. Smith developed more recipes and eventually bought out his former employer, restaurant owner Marie Nordquist.

Today, the *Marie's* brand is owned by Campbell and is the No. 1 selling refrigerated salad dressing in America, with 22 varieties of salad dressings and fruit glazes sold nationally, in addition to a new line of dips. When you try the following recipes, you'll discover that the possibilities for great taste are endless with *Marie's* Dressings and Glazes.

MARIE'S SALAD DRESSING BILLBOARD, CIRCA 1969.

Buffalo Wings

12 **chicken wings (about 2 pounds)**
2 **tablespoons hot pepper sauce**
2 **tablespoons margarine** *or* **butter**
   Celery sticks
   Refrigerated MARIE'S Chunky Blue Cheese Dressing and Dip

- Cut wing tips off at joint and discard; cut each wing in half at joint.
- On rack in broiler pan, arrange wings. Broil 6 inches from heat 25 minutes or until chicken is no longer pink and juices run clear, turning occasionally. Transfer to serving platter.
- Meanwhile, in 1-quart saucepan over medium heat, heat hot pepper sauce and margarine until margarine is melted, stirring often. Drizzle over wings. Serve with celery sticks and dressing for dipping.

Makes 24 Appetizers	Prep Time: 10 Minutes
	Cook Time: 25 Minutes

Blueberry-Peach Sundaes

¾ **cup MARIE'S Glaze for Peaches**
¼ **teaspoon almond extract**
2 **cups vanilla nonfat frozen yogurt**
2 **cups sliced fresh nectarines** *or* **peaches (about 2 medium)**
1 **cup fresh blueberries**

- In small bowl, combine glaze and extract; set aside.
- In 6 dessert dishes, spoon ⅓ cup yogurt. Divide nectarines and blueberries among dishes. Spoon 2 tablespoons glaze mixture over fruit and yogurt. Serve immediately.

Makes 6 Servings	Prep Time: 10 Minutes

These spicy fried chicken wings originated in Buffalo, New York, where they are served by the bucketful in restaurants and bars. Celery sticks and blue cheese dressing always accompany the wings.

TORTELLINI SALAD

8 ounces frozen cheese-filled tortellini (about 2 cups)
½ cup refrigerated MARIE'S ZESTY Fat Free Italian Vinaigrette
1 small cucumber, diced (about 1 cup)
1 medium tomato, diced (about 1 cup)
1 green onion, sliced (about 2 tablespoons)
   Assorted salad greens, optional

- Cook tortellini according to package directions. Drain in colander. In medium bowl, toss hot tortellini with vinaigrette; cool 10 minutes.
- Add cucumber, tomato and onion; toss gently to coat. Serve at room temperature or cover and refrigerate until serving time. Serve on salad greens. If desired, garnish with *plum tomato* and *fresh sage.*

MAKES ABOUT 4½ CUPS OR 4 MAIN-DISH SERVINGS	PREP TIME: 30 MINUTES

CHICKEN AND PASTA SALAD

¾ cup refrigerated MARIE'S Creamy Ranch Dressing and Dip
18 medium cherry tomatoes, halved
1 medium cucumber, peeled, halved lengthwise, seeded and sliced
2 thin wedges red onion, separated
3 tablespoons chopped fresh parsley
2 cans (5 ounces *each*) SWANSON Premium Chunk White Chicken, drained
3 cups cooked corkscrew macaroni (about 2½ cups dry)

- In large bowl, combine dressing, tomatoes, cucumber, onion and parsley. Add chicken and macaroni; toss gently to coat. Cover; refrigerate at least 4 hours before serving. If desired, garnish with *fresh basil* and *additional red onion.*

MAKES ABOUT 7 CUPS OR 5 MAIN-DISH SERVINGS	PREP TIME: 20 MINUTES CHILL TIME: 4 HOURS

TORTELLINI SALAD *(top),*
CHICKEN AND PASTA SALAD *(bottom)*

GLAZED FRUIT SALAD

1 **can (about 11 ounces) mandarin orange segments, drained**
1 **cup seedless green *or* red grapes**
1 **cup sliced fresh strawberries**
2 **medium bananas, sliced**
1 **medium apple, cored and diced**
½ **cup MARIE'S Creamy Glaze for Bananas**
½ **cup miniature marshmallows (optional)**
¼ **cup flaked coconut, toasted (optional)**

- In large bowl, combine fruit and glaze; toss to coat. Serve immediately. Or, cover and refrigerate. Just before serving, gently stir in marshmallows and coconut. If desired, garnish with *fresh orange mint.*

MAKES ABOUT 5½ CUPS OR 5 SIDE-DISH SERVINGS	PREP TIME: 15 MINUTES

STRAWBERRY ANGEL DESSERT

1 **package (about 14 ounces) angel food cake mix**
4 **cups sliced fresh strawberries (about 1 quart)**
1 **jar (14 ounces) MARIE'S Glaze for Strawberries**
1½ **teaspoons lemon juice**
¾ **cup thawed frozen whipped topping**

- Prepare cake according to package directions. Cool.
- In bowl, combine berries, glaze and lemon juice.
- With serrated knife, cut cake in *half* horizontally. Spoon *two thirds* of berry mixture on bottom cake layer. Top with remaining layer; spoon remaining berry mixture on top. Serve with topping.

MAKES 12 SERVINGS	PREP TIME: 30 MINUTES
	BAKE & COOL TIME: 3 HOURS

TWO POPULAR MARIE'S FRUIT GLAZES

GRAVY DAYS

Founded by the Frenchman Alphonse Biardot, the Franco-American Company was one of America's premier gourmet food purveyors in the early 1900s, having produced a line of widely known soups and gravies. In 1917, the products of the Franco-American Foods Company were added to the Campbell family of products and the rest, as they say, is gravy!

With *Franco-American* gravies, delicious suppers are only minutes away when you prepare these family-pleasing recipes.

EASY BEEF STIR-FRY

1 **pound boneless beef sirloin** *or* **top round steak, ¾ inch thick**
2 **tablespoons vegetable oil**
2 **cups fresh broccoli flowerets**
1½ **cups sliced fresh mushrooms (about 4 ounces)**
2 **green onions, cut diagonally into 2-inch pieces (about ½ cup)**
1 **can (10¼ ounces) FRANCO-AMERICAN Beef Gravy**
1 **tablespoon soy sauce**
4 **cups hot cooked rice**

- Slice beef across the grain into thin strips.
- In 10-inch skillet or wok over medium-high heat, in *1 tablespoon* hot oil, stir-fry *half* of the beef until browned. Remove; set aside. Repeat with remaining beef.
- Reduce heat to medium. In same skillet, in remaining *1 tablespoon* hot oil, stir-fry broccoli, mushrooms and green onions until tender-crisp.
- Stir in gravy and soy sauce. Heat to boiling. Return beef to skillet. Heat through, stirring occasionally. Serve over rice with *additional soy sauce.*

Makes 4 Main-Dish Servings	Prep Time: 15 Minutes
	Cook Time: 20 Minutes

Stir-frying is an Oriental cooking technique in which pieces of meat, poultry, seafood and/or vegetables are cooked quickly over high heat with constant stirring. This method requires a minimum amount of fat and results in food that is crisply tender. Traditionally, a wok is used, but a large deep skillet also works well.

1968
ADVERTISEMENT

HOT TURKEY SANDWICHES

2 tablespoons margarine *or* butter
2 small carrots, thinly sliced diagonally (about ½ cup)
1 medium onion, chopped (about ½ cup)
¼ cup sliced celery
¾ teaspoon chopped fresh thyme leaves *or* ¼ teaspoon
    dried thyme leaves, crushed
1 can (10½ ounces) FRANCO-AMERICAN Turkey Gravy
  Sliced cooked turkey (about ½ pound)
4 diagonally sliced pieces Italian bread

- In 2-quart saucepan over medium heat, in hot margarine, cook carrots, onion, celery and thyme until tender, stirring occasionally.
- Stir in gravy. Heat to boiling. Add turkey. Heat through, stirring occasionally. Divide turkey and gravy mixture evenly among bread slices. If desired, serve with *apples* and *grapes;* garnish with *fresh thyme.*

MAKES 4 MAIN-DISH SERVINGS	PREP TIME: 10 MINUTES
	COOK TIME: 10 MINUTES

LEMON CHICKEN PRIMAVERA

1 tablespoon margarine *or* butter
1 pound skinless, boneless chicken breasts, cut into strips
1 can (10½ ounces) FRANCO-AMERICAN Chicken Gravy
1 bag (16 ounces) frozen vegetable combination
3 cloves garlic, minced
2 tablespoons lemon juice
½ teaspoon dried basil leaves, crushed
⅛ teaspoon pepper
4 cups hot cooked spaghetti (about 8 ounces dry)

- In 10-inch skillet over medium-high heat, in hot margarine, cook *half* of the chicken until browned, stirring often. Remove; set aside. Repeat with remaining chicken.
- In same skillet, combine gravy, vegetables, garlic, lemon juice, basil and pepper. Heat to boiling. Reduce heat to low. Cover; cook 10 minutes or until vegetables are tender, stirring occasionally. Return chicken to skillet. Heat through, stirring occasionally. Serve over spaghetti.

MAKES 4 MAIN-DISH SERVINGS	PREP TIME: 10 MINUTES
	COOK TIME: 20 MINUTES

RECIPE INDEX

Recipes by Product Index

EMERGENCY SUBSTITUTIONS

When a recipe calls for:	You may substitute:
Bacon, cooked and crumbled, 1 slice	1 tablespoon bottled bacon pieces
Bread crumbs, dry, ¼ cup	¾ cup soft bread crumbs, ¼ cup cracker crumbs, ¼ cup cornflake crumbs *or* ⅔ cup rolled oats
Buttermilk, 1 cup	1 tablespoon lemon juice *or* vinegar *plus* enough milk to make 1 cup (Let stand 5 minutes before using.)
Chicken, cooked and cubed, 1½ to 2 cups	2 cans (5 ounces *each*) Swanson Premium Chunk White Chicken *or* Turkey, drained
Cornstarch (for thickening), 1 tablespoon	2 tablespoons all-purpose flour *or* 2 teaspoons quick-cooking tapioca
Cream, heavy *or* whipping, 1 cup whipped and sweetened	2 cups thawed frozen whipped topping
Cream, sour, 1 cup	1 cup plain yogurt
Garlic, 1 clove	⅛ teaspoon garlic powder *or* minced dried garlic *or* ½ teaspoon bottled minced garlic
Ginger, fresh, minced, 1 tablespoon	¼ teaspoon ground ginger
Half-and-half, 1 cup	2 tablespoons margarine *or* butter, melted, *plus* enough milk to make 1 cup
Herbs, fresh, chopped, 1 tablespoon	1 teaspoon dried herbs, crushed
Honey, ¼ cup	¼ cup light corn syrup
Margarine, 1 cup	1 cup butter *or* 1 cup vegetable shortening *plus* ¼ teaspoon salt, if desired
Milk, fresh, whole, 1 cup	1 cup 2%, 1% *or* skim milk, *or* ½ cup evaporated milk *plus* ½ cup water
Mustard, prepared (in cooked mixtures), 1 tablespoon	1 teaspoon dry mustard
Mustard, prepared (as a spread/dip), 1 tablespoon	½ teaspoon dry mustard *plus* 2 teaspoons vinegar
Onion, 1 small, chopped (¼ cup)	1 teaspoon onion powder *or* 1 tablespoon minced dried onion, rehydrated
Pepper, ground red (cayenne), ⅛ teaspoon	4 drops hot pepper sauce
Poultry seasoning, 1 teaspoon	¾ teaspoon dried sage leaves, crushed, *plus* ¼ teaspoon dried thyme leaves, crushed
Sugar, granulated, ½ cup	½ cup packed brown sugar
Zucchini, sliced, 1 cup	1 cup sliced summer squash

STORING PERISHABLE FOODS

Follow these guidelines for storing perishable foods in the refrigerator or freezer.

- Raw meat and poultry should be wrapped securely so juices do not leak and contaminate other foods or surfaces. Since repeated handling can introduce bacteria to meat and poultry, it's best to leave the product in the store wrap unless the wrap is torn. Use plastic bags *over* commercial packaging.
- Date purchased food items and be sure to use them within the recommended time.
- Eggs should be stored in their carton in the refrigerator, not in the door.
- Arrange items in the refrigerator or freezer to allow air to circulate evenly.

FOOD STORAGE CHART*

These short but safe storage time limits will help keep refrigerated food from spoiling. The time limits given for frozen foods are to maintain peak flavor and texture.

Product	Refrigerator (40°F.)	Freezer (0°F.)
Eggs		
Fresh, in shell	3 weeks	Don't freeze
Raw yolks, whites	2-4 days	1 year
Hard-cooked	1 week	Don't freeze well
Soups & Stews		
Vegetable or meat-added	3-4 days	2-3 months
Meats & Poultry		
Beef roasts	3-5 days	6-12 months
Beef steaks	3-5 days	6-12 months
Lamb chops	3-5 days	6-9 months
Pork chops	3-5 days	4-6 months
Pork roasts	3-5 days	4-6 months
Stew meat—beef, lamb or pork	1-2 days	3-4 months
Ham, canned, label says "keep refrigerated"	6-9 months	Don't freeze
Ham, fully cooked, slices	3-4 days	1-2 months
Ground beef, lamb, pork, poultry or mixtures of them	1-2 days	3-4 months
Sausage, raw—beef, pork or poultry	1-2 days	1-2 months
Smoked breakfast links or patties	7 days	1-2 months
Bacon	7 days	1 month
Chicken or turkey, whole	1-2 days	1 year
Chicken or turkey pieces	1-2 days	9 months
Cooked Meats & Poultry		
Meat or meat mixtures	3-4 days	2-3 months
Gravy or meat broth	1-2 days	2-3 months
Poultry mixtures	3-4 days	4-6 months
Poultry pieces, plain	3-4 days	4 months
Poultry pieces covered with broth/gravy	1-2 days	6 months

*Source: U.S. Department of Agriculture—Food Safety and Inspection Service.

FOOD EQUIVALENTS

Bread & Cookies	2 slices white bread	1 cup soft crumbs
	8-ounce package dried bread crumbs	2½ cups
	1 pound loaf bread	14 to 20 slices
	14 square graham crackers	1 cup fine crumbs
	22 vanilla wafers	1 cup fine crumbs
	28 saltine crackers	1 cup fine crumbs
Dairy	1 pound margarine *or* butter	2 cups *or* 4 sticks
	¼ pound stick margarine *or* butter	8 tablespoons
	1 cup heavy *or* whipping cream	2 cups whipped
	4-ounce container whipped topping, thawed	1¾ cups
	8 ounces cream cheese	1 cup
	1 pound Swiss *or* Cheddar cheese	4 cups shredded
	4 ounces blue cheese, crumbled	1 cup
	4 ounces Parmesan *or* Romano cheese	1¼ cups grated
	1 large egg	3 tablespoons beaten egg
Fruits	1 medium apple	about 1 cup sliced
	1 pound apples	3 medium
	1 medium banana	about ⅓ cup mashed
	1 pound bananas	3 medium
	1 pint blueberries	3 cups
	12-ounce package whole cranberries	3 cups
	1 medium lemon	about 2 tablespoons juice / about 2 teaspoons shredded peel
	1 medium orange	⅓ to ½ cup juice
	1 large pineapple	about 4 cups cubed
	1 pint strawberries	about 3½ cups whole / about 2¼ cups sliced
Noodles, Pasta & Rice	3 ounces dry medium noodles (3 cups)	about 3 cups cooked
	8 ounces dry elbow macaroni	about 4 cups cooked
	8 ounces dry spaghetti	about 4 cups cooked
	1 cup uncooked regular long-grain rice	about 3 cups cooked
	1 cup uncooked quick-cooking rice	about 2 cups cooked
Vegetables	1 pound green beans, cut into 1-inch pieces	about 3 cups
	1 large bunch broccoli (1½ pounds)	5 cups flowerets
	1 small head cauliflower (1½ pounds)	about 4 cups flowerets
	1 pound cabbage	about 4 cups shredded
	1 medium carrot	about ½ cup shredded
	1 rib celery	about ½ cup sliced
	1 pound mushrooms	3 cups sliced
	4 ounces snow peas	about 1 cup
	1 large green pepper	about 1 cup chopped
	1 pound all-purpose potatoes	3 medium
	1 medium green onion, sliced	about 2 tablespoons
	1 pound yellow onions	5 to 6 medium
	1 pound tomatoes	3 medium

WEIGHTS & MEASURES

Solid Measurements

dash = pinch

generous dash = large pinch (about $\frac{1}{16}$ teaspoon)

3 teaspoons = 1 tablespoon

4 tablespoons = $\frac{1}{4}$ cup

5$\frac{1}{3}$ tablespoons = $\frac{1}{3}$ cup

8 tablespoons = $\frac{1}{2}$ cup

10$\frac{2}{3}$ tablespoons = $\frac{2}{3}$ cup

12 tablespoons = $\frac{3}{4}$ cup

16 tablespoons = 1 cup

1 ounce = 28.35 grams

1 pound = 453.59 grams

1 gram = 0.035 ounce

1 kilogram = 2.2 pounds

Liquid Measurements

1 tablespoon = $\frac{1}{2}$ fluid ounce

2 tablespoons = 1 fluid ounce

1 cup = 8 fluid ounces

1 cup = $\frac{1}{2}$ pint

2 cups = 1 pint = 16 fluid ounces

2 pints = 1 quart = 32 fluid ounces

4 quarts = 1 gallon = 128 fluid ounces

8 quarts = 1 peck

2 gallons = 1 peck

4 pecks = 1 bushel

Useful Equivalents

$\frac{1}{8}$ teaspoon = 0.5 milliliter (mL)

$\frac{1}{4}$ teaspoon = 1 milliliter (mL)

$\frac{1}{2}$ teaspoon = 2 milliliters (mL)

1 teaspoon = 5 milliliters (mL)

1 tablespoon = 15 milliliters (mL)

$\frac{1}{4}$ cup = 2 fluid ounces = 50 milliliters (mL)

$\frac{1}{3}$ cup = 3 fluid ounces = 75 milliliters (mL)

$\frac{1}{2}$ cup = 4 fluid ounces =125 milliliters (mL)

1 cup = 8 fluid ounces = 250 milliliters (mL)

1 quart = 946.4 milliliters (mL)

1 liter = 1.06 quart